KEW POCKETBOOKS

PALMS

Introduction by William J. Baker
Curated by Gina Fullerlove

Kew Publishing
Royal Botanic Gardens, Kew

KEW HOLDS ONE OF THE LARGEST COLLECTIONS of botanical literature, art and archive material in the world. The library comprises 185,000 monographs and rare books, around 150,000 pamphlets, 5,000 serial titles and 25,000 maps. The Archives contain vast collections relating to Kew's long history as a global centre of plant information and a nationally important botanic garden including 7 million letters, lists, field notebooks, diaries and manuscript pages.

The Illustrations Collection comprises 200,000 watercolours, oils, prints and drawings, assembled over the last 200 years, forming an exceptional visual record of plants and fungi. Works include those of the great masters of botanical illustration such as Ehret, Redouté and the Bauer brothers, Thomas Duncanson, George Bond and Walter Hood Fitch. Our special collections include historic and contemporary originals prepared for *Curtis's Botanical Magazine*, the work of Margaret Meen, Thomas Baines, Margaret Mee, Joseph Hooker's Indian sketches, Edouard Morren's bromeliad paintings, 'Company School' works commissioned from Indian artists by Roxburgh, Wallich, Royle and others, and the Marianne North Collection, housed in the gallery named after her in Kew Gardens.

H.T. del. et sc. 1840.

Palmaceæ.
The Palm Tribe.

Day & Son, Lith.rs to The Queen.

INTRODUCTION

———————

PALMS ARE ARGUABLY ONE OF THE MOST ICONIC
botanical symbols. Their bold structure, distilled in the
stereotype to an unbranched, pillar-like trunk topped with
a crown of enormous leaves, is embedded in minds and
cultures worldwide. Almost everybody knows what a palm is,
even if they do not realise it. But this symbolic simplicity is
deceptive. Scratch its surface and you will find breathtaking
diversity in species, form and biology, and discover the
endless ways that palms support human livelihoods.

Palms belong to the plant family Arecaceae (also known
as Palmae, an alternative, more obvious name). They are
essentially tropical. Their iconic structure has an Achilles
heel: they cannot survive freezing, as it causes such
catastrophic damage to their water and nutrient conducting
vessels. Today almost all species are found within the tropics
and subtropics, exceptions being a few hardy species that
occur as far north as southern France and as far south as
the Chatham Islands near New Zealand. In deeper time,
when the planet was warmer, palms ranged more widely and
reached Greenland and Antarctica. Fifty million years ago,
palms even clogged the Thames estuary in London!

Almost 2,600 palm species are known to Western science, with more new species discovered every year. More than 700 of these species are found in the Americas. In the Amazon, six out of the ten commonest tree species are palms. There may be more than five billion individuals of the number one species, the açai palm (*Euterpe precatoria*). Palms are fundamental to the functioning of the forest itself. South America is also home to bizarre stilt-rooted palms such as *Iriartea deltoidea*. Its enormous cone of prop roots resemble legs, and prompted the myth that palms wander around the rainforest.

The Asia-Pacific region is home to more than 1,500 palm species, with many of these restricted to single islands within the region's archipelagos. Here, we find a wealth of climbing palms (rattans) as well as elegant fan palms (*Licuala*) and curious miniature palmlets (such as *Pinanga* and *Calyptrocalyx*) that are abundant in forest understories. In contrast, the continent of Africa has only 66 palm species, perhaps due to great extinctions in the past. All the same, African palms s are important, and include raffia palms (*Raphia*) and the now infamous oil palm (*Elaeis guineensis*). Paradoxically, more than 200 palm species grow in adjacent Madagascar. Almost all of these palms are endemic (they do not grow naturally anywhere else).

Palms' unique construction and their ability to build massive stems bearing weighty structures has allowed them to break many botanical records. The largest leaf in the world, measuring over 25 m / 82 ft, belongs to *Raphia regalis* from Africa. The largest inflorescence is produced by the talipot palm (*Corypha umbraculifera*). Its giant candelabra, some 8 m / 26 ft tall, emerges above the leaves to bear 24 million flowers on branches that can measure 9 m / 29 ft or more in total length. Exhausted by this effort, the talipot literally flowers itself to death. Most famous of all palm records is the largest seed in the world, produced by the Seychelles double coconut (*Lodoicea maldivica*), which can weigh up to 20 kg / 44 lbs. Palms are not just giants; they are hugely diverse in size and growth form. There are minute almost herb-like palms, stemless shrub palms, crawling palms with trunks prostrate to the ground, and vigorous climbers with stems that can scramble to the rainforest canopy. Those who complain that all palms look the same simply aren't looking carefully.

The marvel of palm structure is not just a botanical curiosity; their unique build underpins their immense usefulness to humans. Their long, straight, easily split stems lend themselves to use in construction, and their leaves to use as thatch, or for weaving. Palms can be immensely productive, producing edible or oily fruits and seeds (such as coconuts and dates), building up edible starch (sago) in their stems, or weeping copious sap that can be fermented to alcohol or boiled down to sugar. Only grasses and legumes rival them economically, but while palms cannot compete as large-scale production crops, they win hands down for multiplicity of uses at a subsistence level, providing essential resources to some of the world's poorest communities. The palm truly earns its moniker 'the tree of life'.

This makes it all the more important that we protect palms from extinction. Like all life on Earth, palms face existential threats from habitat loss and climate change and their value to humans increases their risks, as they are exploited in a targeted way. In Madagascar, where forest destruction and poverty drive extinction risk to terrifying levels, more than 80 per cent of palm species are threatened – the world is losing palm species before they are even known to science.

Kew scientists have studied palms for more than a century. In Victorian times, they were amply showcased in Kew's groundbreaking economic botany museums and, of course, the Palm House, a glass cathedral for the tropics. Joseph Dalton Hooker, Kew's second director, classified the palms in 1883, a treatment scarcely challenged for 100 years. Since the mid-1970s, a focused programme of research has brought to light a wealth of new knowledge on species diversity, classification, evolution, natural history, uses and conservation. We continue this tradition to this day, using our unique collections in cutting-edge scientific research.

In this time of unprecedented biodiversity crisis, the living world needs advocates. This is as true for palms as for any other living thing. Through its reproductions of botanical art drawn from Kew's immense collections, this book demonstrates the wonders of palms and encourages you to advocate for them. We hope you will experience the thrill felt by those pioneering botanists and artists as they explored for palms and learnt their uses – the same thrill that Kew scientists feel today, more urgently, as we explore what is left of the world's rainforests, discovering palms just in the nick of time.

William J. Baker
Head, Comparative Plant & Fungal Biology,
Royal Botanic Gardens, Kew

Tenga, Setna.
Malabarica
Arabica
Lingua Bramanica antiqua

Areca catechu

betel palm, 'The Drunken Date'

———————

from John Gerard *The Herball;*
or Generall Historie of Plantes, 1636

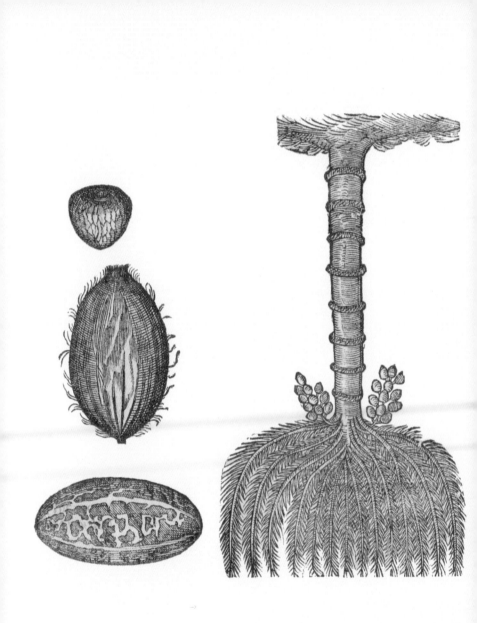

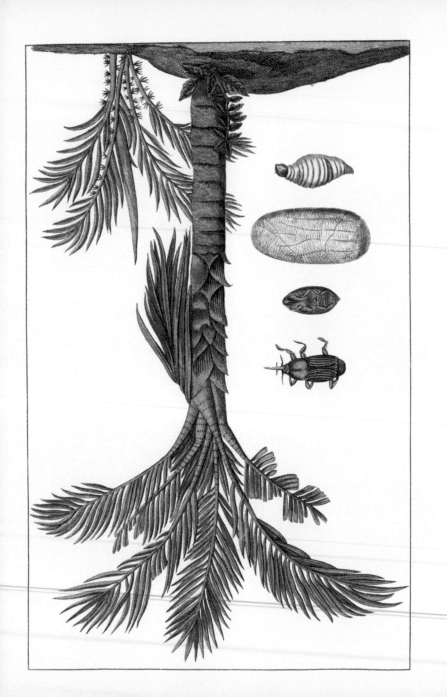

Metroxylon sagu

sago palm

from Georgius Everhardus Rumphius
Herbarium Amboinense, 1750

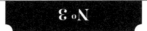

Elaeis guineensis

African oil palm

---

from Nicolaus Joseph von Jacquin
Selectarum Stirpium Americanarum Historia,
1780-81

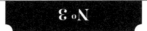

N⁰ 3

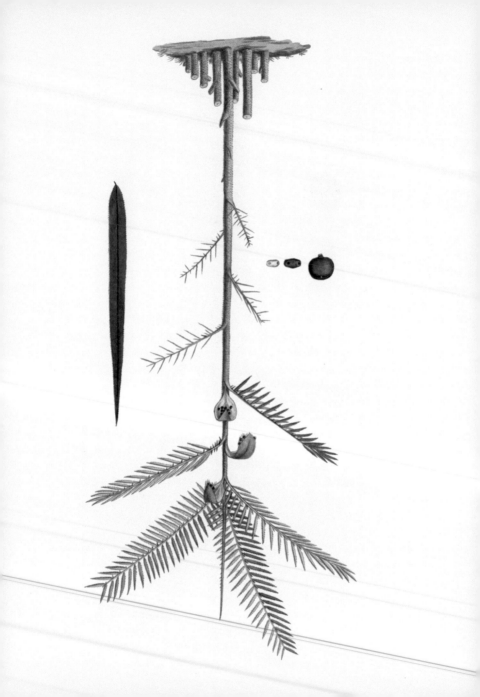

Nº 4

Bactris guineensis

Guinea bactris, Tobago cane

_____

from Nicolaus Joseph von Jacquin
Selectarum Stirpium Americanarum Historia,
1780–81

Arenga pinnata

sugar palm

by unknown artist from the
George Finlayson Collection, Kew, c.1820

Nº 5

Wallichia caryotoides

chilputta, walizong,
saingpa, kuang denj

---

by unknown Indian artist commissioned
by William Roxburgh, Kew Collection, c.1800

Oncosperma tigillarium

nibong palm

by unknown artist from the
George Finlayson Collection, Kew, c.1820

N⁰ 8

Calamus gracilis

by unknown Indian artist commissioned
by William Roxburgh, Kew Collection, c.1800

Calamus viminalis

rattan, chair bottom cane

by unknown Indian artist commissioned
by William Roxburgh, Kew Collection, c.1800

№ 9

Calamus melanochaetes
rattan

———————

by unknown Indian artist from
William Griffith and John McClelland
Palms of British East India, 1850

№ 11

Licuala peltata

fan palm

———

by unknown Indian artist commissioned
by William Roxburgh, Kew Collection, c.1800

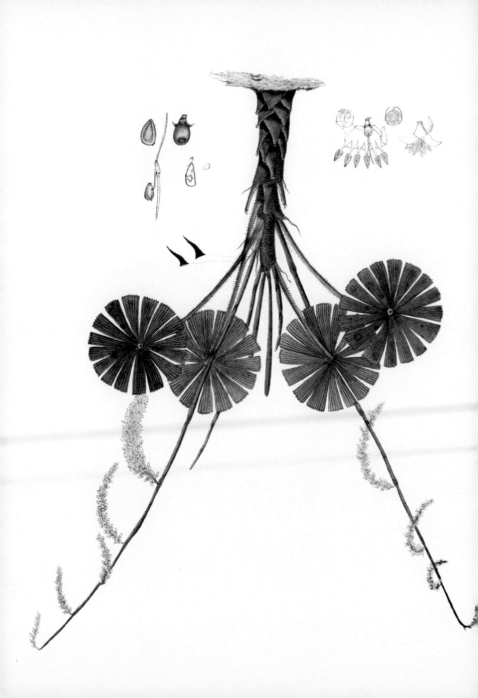

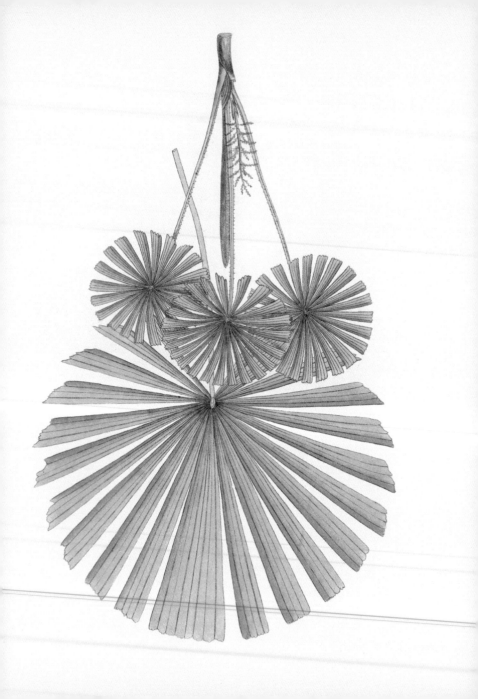

№ 12

Licuala longipes

fan palm

by unknown Indian artist from
William Griffith and John McClelland
Palms of British East India, 1850

N⁰ 13

Trachycarpus martianus

Himalayan fan palm

_____

probably by Vishnupersaud
from Wallich Collection, Kew, c.1825

Livistona chinensis

Chinese fan palm, fountain palm

––––––––––

by unknown Asian artist, Company Art,
Kew Collection, 18th century

Livistona jenkinsiana

Major Jenkins' fan palm

---

by unknown Indian artist from
William Griffith and John McClelland
Palms of British East India, 1850

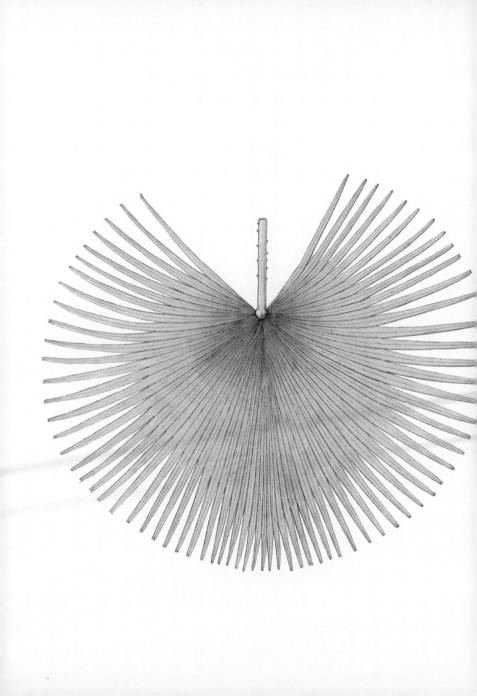

Corypha taliera

by unknown Indian artist from
William Griffith and John McClelland
Palms of British East India, 1850

Pinanga gracilis

by unknown Indian artist from
William Griffith and John McClelland
Palms of British East India, 1850

No 17

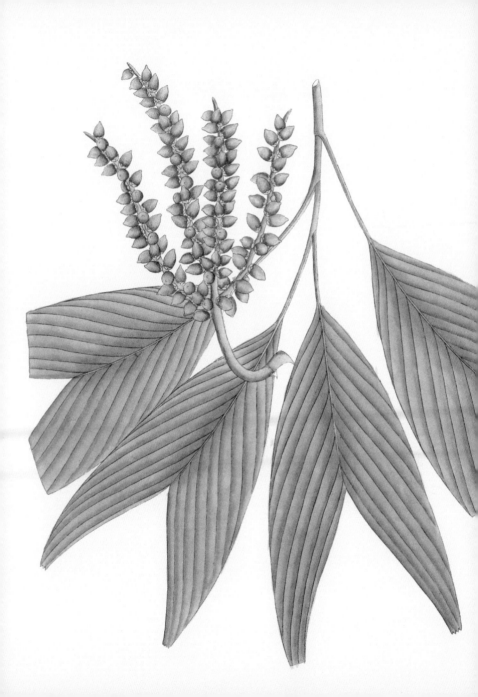

Oncosperma horridum

mountain nibong palm

_____

by unknown Indian artist from
William Griffith and John McClelland
Palms of British East India, 1850

No 19

Licuala triphylla

fan palm

_____

by unknown Indian artist from
William Griffith and John McClelland
Palms of British East India, 1850

N⁰ 20

Caryota mitis

Burmese fishtail palm

———————

by unknown Indian artist from
William Griffith and John McClelland
Palms of British East India, 1850

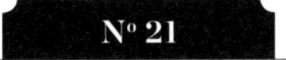

Eugeissona tristis

bertam, bertam palm

---

by unknown Indian artist from
William Griffith and John McClelland
Palms of British East India, 1850

Actinorhytis calapparia

calappa palm

by unknown Indian artist from
William Griffith and John McClelland
Palms of British East India, 1850

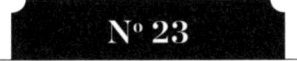

N° 23

Nypa fruticans

nipa, mangrove palm

———————

by unknown Asian artist,
Company Art, Kew Collection, c. 1800

№ 24

Trachycarpus fortunei
Chusan palm,
Chinese windmill palm

————

by unknown Chinese artist,
Robert Fortune Collection, Kew, c.1850

N⁰ 25

Coccothrinax barbadensis

latanier, latanier balai

———————

by Pieter de Pannemaeker from
Oswald Charles Eugene Marie Ghislain de Kerchove
de Denterghem *Les Palmiers*, 1878

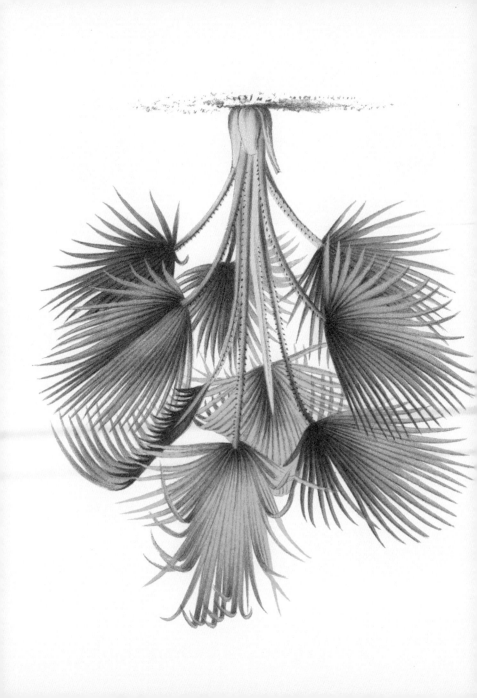

N° 26

Salacca affinis

red salak

by unknown Indian artist from
William Griffith and John McClelland
Palms of British East India, 1850

Mauritiella armata

from Karl Friedrich Philipp von Martius
Historia Naturalis Palmarum, 1823–53

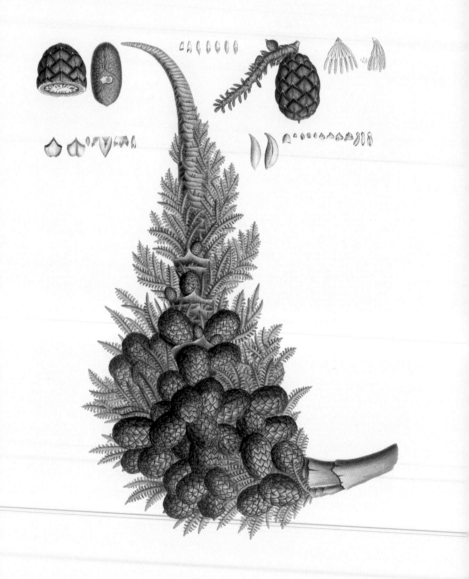

N° 28

Raphia taedigera
yolilla

from Karl Friedrich Philipp von Martius
Historia Naturalis Palmarum, 1823-53

N° 29

Ptychosperma elegans

solitaire palm

by Ferdinand Bauer
from Karl Friedrich Philipp von Martius
Historia Naturalis Palmarum, 1823–53

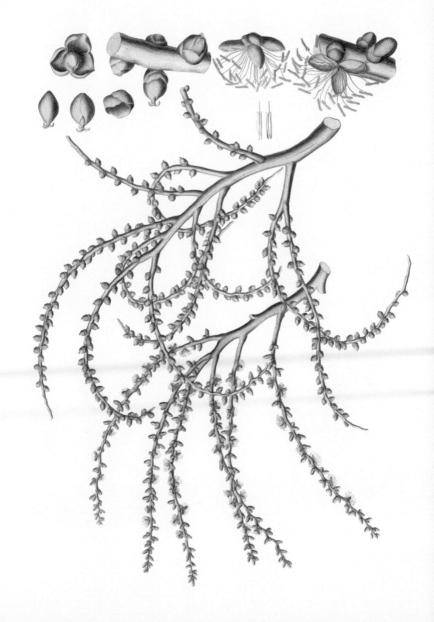

Hyospathe elegans

from Karl Friedrich Philipp von Martius
Historia Naturalis Palmarum, 1823–53

No 30

Livistona humilis

by Ferdinand Bauer
from Karl Friedrich Philipp von Martius
Historia Naturalis Palmarum, 1823–53

Livistona inermis

from Karl Friedrich Philipp von Martius
Historia Naturalis Palmarum, 1823–53

N° 32

Oenocarpus distichus

babaca palm

---

from Karl Friedrich Philipp von Martius
Historia Naturalis Palmarum, 1823–53

N° 33

Iriartea deltoidea

bombona, pambil, pona palm

from Karl Friedrich Philipp von Martius
Historia Naturalis Palmarum, 1823–53

Hyphaene thebaica

doum palm, gingerbread tree

———————

from Karl Friedrich Philipp von Martius
Historia Naturalis Palmarum, 1823–53

N° 36

Chamaedorea linearis

whale tail palm

_____

from Karl Friedrich Philipp von Martius
Historia Naturalis Palmarum, 1823–53

Astrocaryum aculeatum, tucumã
Bactris hirta var. *pectinata*
Bactris hirta

from Karl Friedrich Philipp von Martius
Historia Naturalis Palmarum, 1823–53

Lodoicea maldivica

coco de mer, double coconut

from *Curtis's Botanical Magazine*, 1827

Borassus flabellifer

Palmyra palm

_____

by Marianne North
from Marianne North Collection, Kew, 1870

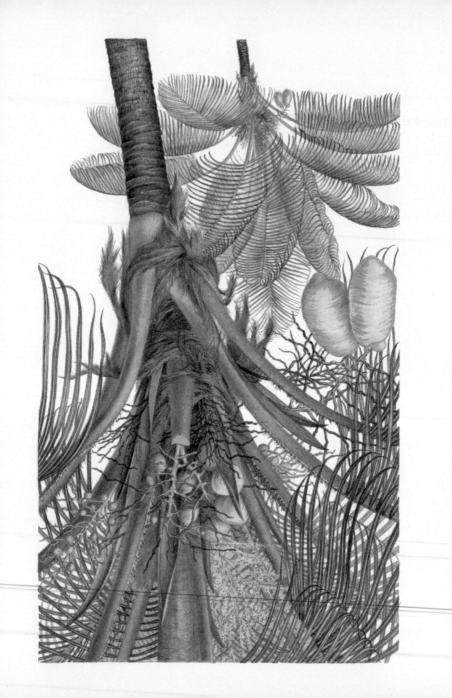

Cocos nucifera

coconut palm

———————

by Christabel King
from *Curtis's Botanical Magazine*, 1999

ILLUSTRATION SOURCES

Books and Journals

Dransfield, John and Cooke, David. (1999). *Cocos nucifera. Curtis's Botanical Magazine*. Volume 16/1, plate 355.

Gerard, John. (1636). *The Herball; or Generall Historie of Plantes.* Adam Islip, Joice Norton and Richard Whitakers, London.

Griffith, William and McClelland, John. (1850). *Palms of British East India.* C. A. Serrao, Calcutta.

Hooker, W. J. (1827). *Lodoicea sechellarum. Curtis's Botanical Magazine.* Volume 54, t. 2734.

Jacquin, Nicolaus Joseph von. (1780–81). *Selectarum Stirpium Americanarum Historia.* 3 volumes. In Bibliopolio Novo Aul. & Acad., Manheim.

Kerchove de Denterghem, Oswald Charles Eugene Marie Ghislain de. (1878). *Les Palmiers.* J. Rothschild, Paris.

Martius, Karl Friedrich Philipp von. (1823–53). *Historia Naturalis Palmarum.* 3 volumes. T.O Weigel, Leipzig.

Reede tot Drakestein, Hendrik van. (1678–1703). *Hortus Indicus Malabaricus.* 12 volumes. Sumptibus Joannis van Someren, Joannis van Dyck, Henrici and Theodori Boom, Amsterdam.

Rumphius, Georgius Everhardus. (1750). *Herbarium Amboinense ... in Latinum sermonem Versa Cura et Studio J. Burmanni.* 6 volumes. Apud Meinardum Uytwerf, Amsterdam.

Twining, Elizabeth. (1849–1855). *Illustrations of the Natural Orders of Plants, Arranged in Groups, with Descriptions.* Joseph Cundall (Volume 1), Day & Son (Volume 2), London.

Art Collections

'Company School' drawings and paintings – most given to Kew in 1879 when the museum and library of the East India Company was dispersed, following its inheritance by the India Office of the British government. Collections include:

• William Roxburgh (1751–1815). One of two sets of 'Icones' comprising 2,500 drawings by Indian artists, made 1776–1813, working on the Coromandel Coast and at the Calcutta Botanic Garden, commissioned by Roxburgh. A duplicate set is held by the Central National Herbarium, Botanical Survey of India, in Kolkata's Acharya Jagadish Chandra Bose Indian Botanic Garden.

• Nathaniel Wallich (1786–1854). About 1,000 drawings by named Indian artists, intimately connected to the Herbarium of the East India Company, also known as the Wallich Herbarium, held at Kew, comprising dried plant specimens obtained by Wallich on his travels in the Indian subcontinent.

• George Finlayson (1790–1823). Collection of 71 watercolour and pencil works by unknown artists, many likely to have originated from the East India Company surgeon's travels in Siam (Thailand), Cochin China (Vietnam), and East Indies (1821–22).

Robert Fortune (1812–80). Collection made by Scottish plant collector who travelled extensively in the Far East, often for the Horticultural Society of London, working in China and Japan from 1843 until 1862.

Marianne North (1830–90). Comprising over 800 oils on paper, showing plants in their natural settings, painted by North, who recorded the world's flora during travels from 1871 to 1885, with visits to 16 countries in 5 continents. The main collection is on display in the Marianne North Gallery at Kew Gardens, bequeathed by North and built according to her instructions, first opened in 1882.

ACKNOWLEDGEMENTS

Kew Publishing would like to thank the following for their help with this publication: Kew palm experts, Bill Baker and John Dransfield; Research Associate of the Royal Botanic Gardens, Edinburgh and Kew, Henry Noltie; Editor, *Curtis's Botanical Magazine*, Martyn Rix; in Kew's Library, Art and Archives Fiona Ainsworth, Julia Buckley, Lynn Parker, Craig Brough and Anne Marshall; for digitisation work, Paul Little; for permission to use her illustration on page 90, botanical artist, Christabel King.

FURTHER READING

Dransfield, John, Uhl, Natalie Whitford, Asmussen, Conny B., Baker, William, Harley, Madeline M. Lewis, Carl E. (2008). *Genera Palmarum: The Evolution and Classification of Palms*, 2nd edition. Royal Botanic Gardens, Kew.

Jacquin, Nicolaus Joseph von. (2016). *Selectarum Stirpium Americanarum. Plants of the Americas*, Facsimile edition. The Folio Society, London.

Martius, Karl Friedrich Philipp von, Mohl, Hugo von, Unger, Franz, Lack, Hans Walter. (2010). *The Book of Palms*. Facsimile plates from *Historia Naturalis Palmarum*. Taschen, Köln.

North, Marianne and Mills, Christopher. (2018). *Marianne North: The Kew Collection*. Royal Botanic Gardens, Kew.

Payne, Michelle. (2016). *Marianne North: A Very Intrepid Painter*, revised edition. Royal Botanic Gardens, Kew.

Rumphius, Georgius Everhardus and Beekman, E. M. (2011). *The Ambonese Herbal*. 6 volumes. National Tropical Botanical Garden and Yale University Press, New Haven and London.

Teltscher, Kate. (2020). *Palace of Palms: Tropical Dreams and the Making of Kew*. Picador, London in association with the Royal Botanic Gardens, Kew.

Watt, Alistair. (2017). *Robert Fortune: A Plant Hunter in the Orient*. Royal Botanic Gardens, Kew.

Willis, Kathy and Fry, Carolyn. (2014). *Plants from Roots to Riches*. John Murray, London in association with the Royal Botanic Gardens, Kew.

Online

www.biodiversitylibrary.org The world's largest open access digital library specialising in biodiversity and natural history literature and archives, including many rare books.

www.kew.org Royal Botanic Gardens, Kew website with information on Kew's science, collections and visitor programme.

www.plantsoftheworldonline.org An online database providing authoritative information of the world's flora gathered from the botanical literature published over the last 250 years.

INDEX

First published in 2020
Royal Botanic Gardens, Kew,
Richmond, Surrey, TW9 3AB, UK
www.kew.org

ISBN 978 1 84246 711 4

Distributed on behalf of the Royal Botanic Gardens, Kew in North America by the University of Chicago Press, 1427 East 60th St, Chicago, IL 60637, USA.

British Library Cataloguing in Publication Data
A catalogue record for this book is available from the British Library

Design and page layout: Ocky Murray
Image work: Christine Beard
Production Manager: Jo Pillai
Copy-editing: Michelle Payne

Printed and bound in Italy by Printer Trento srl.

Front cover image: *Livistona chinensis* (see page 39)

Endpapers: World map showing distribution of palms in New and Old Worlds from Karl Friedrich Philipp von Martius *Historia Naturalis Palmarum*, 1823–53.

p2: 'Dattiers de la Plaine Ghizih' by Pieter de Pannemaeker from Oswald Charles Eugene Marie Ghislain de Kerchove de Denterghem *Les Palmiers*, 1878.

p4: Different palms and their plant parts from Elizabeth Twining *Illustrations of the Natural Orders of Plants*, 1855.

p10: *Cocos nucifera*, coconut palm by Anton Jacob Goedkint from Hendrik van Reede tot Drakestein *Hortus Indicus Malabaricus*, 1678

For information or to purchase all Kew titles please visit shop.kew.org/kewbooksonline or email publishing@kew.org

Kew's mission is to be the global resource in plant and fungal knowledge and the world's leading botanic garden.

Kew receives approximately one third of its funding from Government through the Department for Environment, Food and Rural Affairs (Defra). All other funding needed to support Kew's vital work comes from members, foundations, donors and commercial activities, including book sales.

Publishers note about names
The scientific names of the plants featured in this book are current, Kew accepted names at the time of going to press. They may differ from those used in original-source publications. The common names given are those most often used in the English language, or sometimes vernacular names used for the plants in their native countries.

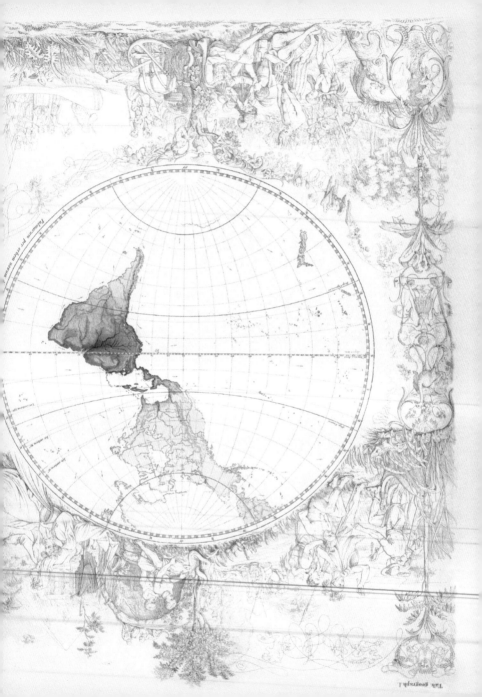